55/1110L

The Living Last Supper

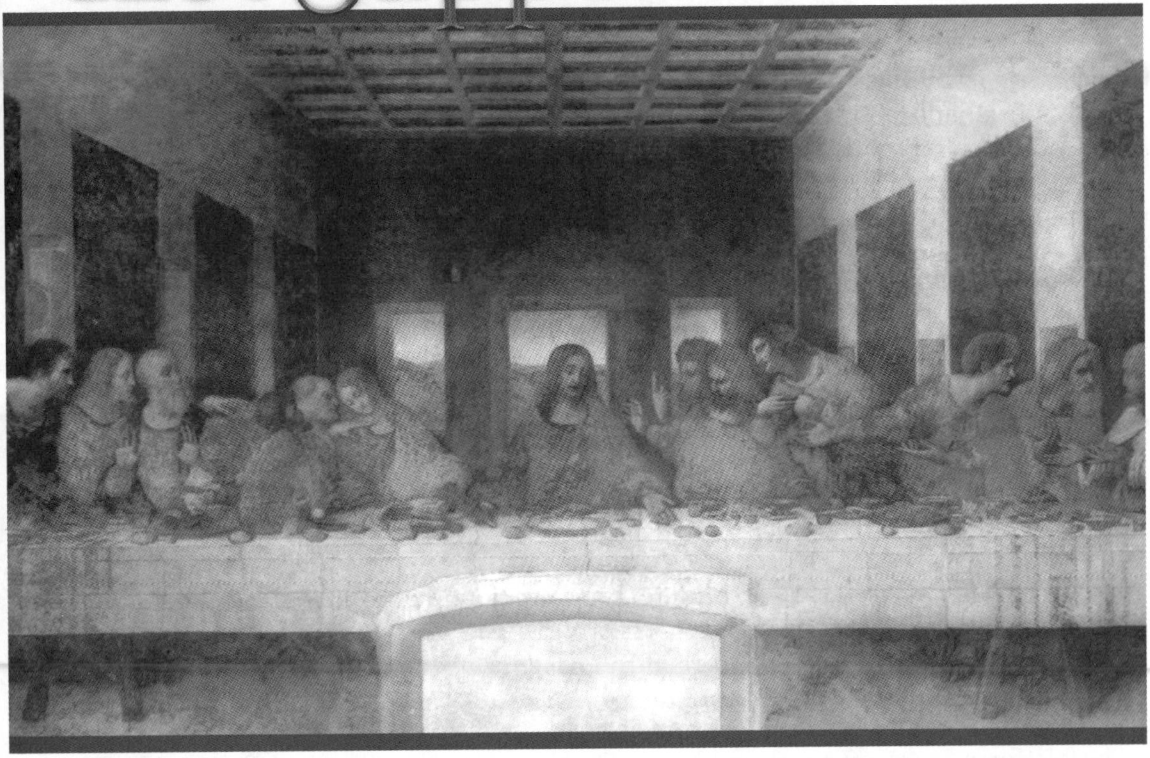

A Dramatic Musical Experience for Holy Week

FOR SATB CHOIR, SPEAKERS AND OPTIONAL SMALL ORCHESTRA

RUTH ELAINE SCHRAM

From the composer

For centuries before Jesus came to earth, each year when the spring harvest began, the Jewish people were instructed to remember the emancipation of Israel from slavery in Egypt by observing Passover. Ritual prayers of blessing were learned and recited. All leaven was removed from the house, a specific set of foods was prepared on dishes used only for this occasion, and a ceremony was performed by each family through which the story of the Exodus was retold. The instructions for the Passover Feast were given to Moses before the Ten Commandments! It pre-dates all other feasts, and its importance was made clear when Jesus chose to celebrate this feast during His last hours.

The Passover Supper is rich with beauty and symbolism, but its significance is lost to many Christians today. The unleavened bread represents the sinless Savior; it is broken and half hidden away, representing His death and burial; it is later uncovered and eaten. Many families involve the children in the story by making a game of hiding and searching for the bread. The Matzo bread used for this ceremony is grilled, so it has stripes that remind us that Jesus was beaten; it has holes in it, which remind us that He was pierced. When Jesus says to His disciples, "This is my body," it gives the bread a whole new level of meaning. The blood of a lamb figures heavily into this ceremony as well. In Egypt, the Israelites painted their door posts with the blood of a spotless lamb. When the angel of death saw this, he "passed over" those homes and spared the first-born from the last of the ten plagues—the plague of death. When John refers to Jesus as "...the Lamb of God who takes away the sins of the world," it becomes clear that the Israelites had been presenting a picture of Jesus' death, burial, and resurrection for 1500 years before His birth by celebrating Passover!

The Living Last Supper is a 35-minute program for Maundy Thursday, Lent or any communion service. It incorporates the Da Vinci painting as a model for the set and is also meant to present a true picture of the Last Supper, which was a celebration of the Passover Feast.

The platform is set up to resemble the Da Vinci painting *The Last Supper.* If desired, a backdrop may be painted to look like windows, etc. (Note: the Production Support CD-ROM [99/2069L] contains a graphic file of the background of Da Vinci's painting. Saved in multiple formats, it may be projected as a backdrop or used to create a custom backdrop.) A long, low table is set lengthwise with thirteen chairs. Jesus sits in the middle with six disciples on either side. The table may be covered with a plain cloth. Candles and candlesticks, goblets, bowls, plates, bunches of grapes, and flat (unleavened) bread (or pita) may be used as props. Additional suggestions for props and staging are also provided (beginning on page 57), but feel free to be creative within the constraints of the set and storyline.

Jesus and the disciples should be dressed in Biblical costumes to resemble the painting as closely as possible. Encourage the men portraying the disciples to forego haircuts and shaving (if feasible) for several weeks/months prior to the production to more closely match the painting and to create an authentic representation of the period.

Each of the disciples has a short monologue based on scripture and historical information. The disciples should stand to deliver the monologues and be placed in such a way that the speaking order will appear random, going from stage left to stage right. The speaking parts are meant to allow us to hear the inner thoughts of each man. When a monologue is being delivered, the rest of the men should freeze until the speaker sits and says, "Is it I?" to Jesus at the end. When he sits, Jesus should look at the disciple and action should resume until the next monologue or musical cue.

Anthems sung by the choir are interspersed throughout the program to underscore the Biblical truths presented by the disciples, to augment their monologues, and to focus on pivotal events in the Biblical story not covered by the drama. Staging suggestions are provided on pages 58-64 for each song indicating whether the action should continue or the cast should freeze. An opportunity is given for your church to celebrate communion if desired. A very effective way to do this is to invite the congregation to process to the table. There, the disciples will give each congregant a piece of unleavened bread and allow them to dip their bread in the cup Jesus holds. (See page 64 for additional suggestions.)

The character of each disciple is based upon the Bible passages where each is mentioned. In some cases, there are discrepancies between gospels as to the names of the twelve men. Where little or no documentation exists about the individual disciple other than his name within the list, the content of the monologue is taken from gospel accounts of events where he was likely to have been present, or with which he would have been familiar. A brief description of each man is provided on page 4 to help the person portraying him in your production develop a character with distinct personality traits.

When God called these twelve men to be His disciples and apostles and to establish the New Testament Church, He chose flawed individuals, people just like you and me, men who were not saints or even finished products, but works in progress; men whose qualities needed to be honed, molded and channeled in positive ways. It is my prayer that God will use this production to remind all of us that He is not yet finished with any of us, and that every one of us is guilty of denying and betraying Him. The most important lesson of this presentation, however, is that His love and mercy covers every contingency, and His will is perfect, even if it is difficult to understand. Just as these twelve exemplary men had a mission given to them to build the New Testament Church on a foundation of love and grace, we are also charged to continue that mission, to love one another and to share the good news of the Messiah.

–Ruth Elaine Schram

For more information about the Passover Feast, visit www.holidays.net/passover/ or www.jewfaq.org/holidaya.htm.

If you are interested in an in-depth look at Passover from a (converted) Jewish perspective, see Zola Levitt ministries at www.levitt.com or www.worshipradio.com/home/ZolaVideo.html.

Cast of Characters

Simon Peter

Stubborn, impulsive, outspoken but sincere, demonstrative. Use large hand gestures.

Andrew, Peter's brother

Under Peter's shadow; more introverted, winsome, steady.

James, the Lesser – son of Alphaeus

Short, perhaps insecure.

James, the son of Zebedee – called the "Son of Thunder"

Boisterous, egotistical. Came from a rich, powerful family.

Matthew, the publican – tax collector

Shrewd businessman, wealthy (by stealing). Wrote the gospel of Matthew.

Simon, the Zealot

Political zealot from Canaan. Tough, opinionated, ambitious, enthusiastic.

Bartholomew/Nathanael

Honest, student of scripture, "true" (devout) Israelite.

Philip

Pragmatic, practical. Later became a missionary.

Thaddaeus/Lebbaeus

(For our purposes) An observer, deep thinker; quiet and introspective.

John, James's brother – the beloved disciple, also a "Son of Thunder"

Has a humble spirit, is emotional and emotive. Wrote the gospel of John.

Thomas

Negative, pessimistic, skeptical. After Jesus' resurrection, he has a change of heart and becomes a bold missionary.

Judas Iscariot

Business-minded treasurer of the group. Emotional, militant, legalistic, opportunistic.

Jesus (non-speaking role)

Female to light candles (optional)

Contents

Set and props suggestions are provided on page 57.
All monologues and staging suggestions are provided on pages 58-64.

Companion Products

55/1116L ....SAB Score
30/2200L ....Small Orchestra Full Score and Parts
Fl., Ob., 2 Clar., Perc., Pno., Vln. 1 & 2, Vla., Cello, Bass
99/2048L........Performance CD
99/2049L........Bulk Performance CDs (10 pak)
99/2050L........Accompaniment CD
99/2051L........SA/TB Part-dominant Rehearsal CDs (reproducible)
99/2069L........Production Support CD-ROM (set and promotional images)
55/1111L ....Performance CD/SATB Score Combination

Overture/Processional

Ruth Elaine Schram

Duration: 1:55

www.lorenz.com

16
cresc.
f
poco rall.
20
a tempo
24
poco rall.
27
mf
ff
a tempo
31
poco rall.
a tempo
rit. e dim.
34
mp
8va

How Great His Love

SATB

Ruth Elaine Schram

Duration: 3:20

www.lorenz.com

12
SA
ry;
How great His
TB
mf
To drink the cup of pain and sor - row; How great His
15
4
love, how great His love for me.
love, how great His love for me. How great His
17
How great the love of God, the Fa - ther, to choose a
love; God, the Fa - ther,

19
plan that sends His on - ly Son to live with
21
us, to walk a - mong us; How great His
23
5
f
love, how great His love for us. How great His
f

25
love, how great His love, that He should
27
6
call us His chil - dren, that He should
29
poco rall.
mf
give Je - sus; How great His
How great His
poco rall.
mf

32
a tempo
love for us,
how great His love for
love for us,
How great His love,
how great His love for
a tempo
34
7
poco rall.
f
us.
How great His
us.
How great His
poco rall.
f
36
a tempo
love, how gen-'rous His com - pas - sion, to meet our
love, His com - pas - sion,
a tempo

38
need before we knew to ask; To call our
40
names, to beck-on us to fol - low; How great His
8
42
love, how great His love for us. How great His

44
love, how great His love, that He should
46
poco rall.
call us His chil - dren, that He should give
poco rall.
9
49
mf
Je - sus.
How great His
How great His
mf

52
a tempo
poco rall.
love,
how great His love for
love for us,
how great His love,
a tempo
poco rall.
54
a tempo
rit. e dim.
mp
us.
How
a tempo
rit. e dim.
57
great His love for us.
mp
p

Monologue: Simon Peter

My name is Simon Peter. One day, my partners and I were cleaning our nets after a long, hard night of fishing. We were tired and discouraged; we had nothing to show for our efforts. Jesus was preaching, as usual, to the many people who followed Him from here to there, listening to His every word. He asked if He could sit in my boat, *(gesture outward)* and I rowed Him out a little so His voice would carry. When He had finished teaching, He asked me to row out a little further and throw my nets in the water again. *(becoming agitated)* I told Him it was pointless; we had worked all night and caught nothing! But, I did as He asked. *(with awe)* And then, astonishingly—so many fish—the nets broke trying to pull them in. *(voice rising)* So many fish—we filled both of our ships until they began to sink under the weight of them!

(bowing head) I fell down on my knees before the Lord, feeling sinful and faithless in His Holy presence. Then He told me I would no longer catch fish, but men. I did not fully understand, but I left my boats, my fish, my livelihood—I left everything to follow Jesus, and I have never looked back.

(looking around the table) Tonight He tells us that one of these twelve men, His faithful disciples, will betray Him. *(loudly)* I vainly promised to follow Him even to death, but *(softly)* He looked right into my eyes and said that before the rooster crows, I will deny Him three times. Deny Him! Am I not the "rock" He called me to be? *(emotionally pained)* Could I lose my Lord, my friend, because I am not strong enough to be faithful? *(sit; to Jesus, quietly)* Is it I?

Monologue: Andrew

I've been known as "Peter's little brother, Andrew" since the day I was born. Years ago I left the fishing business to follow that fiery preacher, John the Baptizer. He was anointed by God to prepare the way for the long-awaited Messiah, *(look at Jesus)* and now I follow Him.

(smiling) I love to bring people to Jesus. I brought my brother to Jesus, *(look at Peter)* and have watched him grow and become a strong leader among us. *(distant; remembering)* I brought the little boy with the lunch of five loaves and two fish to Jesus. *(look to Jesus)* I have even brought Gentiles to meet the Master because He is open and loving to anyone who is searching for the truth.

(sobering) But Jesus has enemies in high places, enemies who would love to silence Him, or even see Him die. And He speaks of a betrayer in our midst. *(prayerfully)* Oh, please do not let it be me who brings sorrow to my Lord! *(sit; barely audible, to Jesus)* Jesus, is it I?

Monologue: James, the Lesser

(a bit reserved) I am James, the Lesser, known as such to describe my stature and to differentiate me from the many other men named James. Since joining Jesus' group of followers, I have seen the most miraculous things! Jesus has the power to calm the sea—even the wind and rain obey His voice. Jesus has power over demons—He has cast out evil spirits and given us the power to do the same in His name. He has the power of healing—He has taken away diseases that people have suffered with for years, even *(in amazement)* from birth. *(with wonder)* Beyond this, He has the power to forgive sin.

(looking at each of several men, studying their faces, end with back to Jesus) And now one of these men at this dinner table, one who eats and drinks with Him, will betray Him. How could anyone doubt that He is the Lord, our Messiah, after walking and talking with Him, after seeing prophecies fulfilled, and miracle after miracle, proof after proof? He has called each of us to follow—*(turn to Jesus)* who could turn away? *(sit)* Is it I?

Is It I?

SATB

Ruth Elaine Schram

Duration: 2:50

www.lorenz.com

11
poco rall.
a tempo
Is it I who will de - ny Him to - night?
Is it I who will de - ny Him to - night?
poco rall.
a tempo
14
mf
We left be-hind the life we knew to fol-low Him, for-
mf
17
sak - ing all to la - bor at His side. We

with urgency
19
left our homes and fam - i - lies, we trav - el with Him con - stant - ly, and
21
cresc.
rall.
now He says that one of us is go - ing to be - tray Him, and that
cresc.
rall.
23
12
f
a tempo
sub. mp
He will be de - nied! Is it I?
f
sub. mp
a tempo

26
Is it I? Is it I who will de - ny Him?
29
cresc.
Could it be e - ven
Would it be, could it be
cresc.
31
mf
poco rall.
to -
me who will de - ny Him to -
e - ven me who will de - ny Him to -
mf
poco rall.

13
a tempo
night?
night, to - night?
To
night, to - night?
a tempo
f
each of us He's been the true Mes - si - ah ful -
fill - ing ev - 'ry prom - ise proph - e - sied.
We've

39
seen first-hand what He can do, we know that ev-'ry word is true, but

41
rall.
now He says that one of us is go-ing to be-tray Him, and that
rall.

43 [14]
a tempo
mf
He will be de-nied. Would it be,
Could it
mf
a tempo

46
could it be
e-ven me
who will de - ny
Him?
be
e - ven
me
who will de - ny
Him?
49
mp
rit.
mp
Is it I?
Is it I?
Is it I who will de -
Is it I?
Is it I?
Is it I
who will de -
mp
rit.
52
pp
ny
Him
to - night?
ny
Him
to - night?
8va
pp
8va

Monologue: James, the son of Zebedee

(with some arrogance) My name is James; *(gesture toward John)* John is my younger brother. We used to work with Peter and Andrew in the fishing industry. Jesus called us to follow Him on the same day that He called Peter, *(look toward Peter)* and we did, thinking that He would establish His kingdom on earth and that we would be His right-hand men.

Jesus calls John and me *(enjoying the title)* "the Sons of Thunder!" *(aside)* Actually, we are the sons of Zebedee, a rich and powerful man in this community who is a personal friend of some of the more influential religious leaders. At one time, I had hoped that this would assure me of a position of power in the new kingdom. In fact, my mother suggested I should sit at Jesus' right hand when He claimed His throne, *(look at John)* and John at His left. *(with authority)* After all, it was we who were invited to the mountain with Jesus, and we saw Him transfigured. *(looking up)* His face shone like the sun, *(with wonder)* and the voice of God spoke out of heaven.

(looking out again) He chose me! He chose each of us. How could one of us betray Him? We have seen His perfect adherence to the law; we have heard the voice of God say, "this is My Son." We have been present during countless miracles, healings—works no mere man could accomplish. *(gesture to John)* Could it be my brother, John? *(look around the table; sit)* Could it be me? *(to Jesus)* Is it I?

Monologue: Matthew

(with strength and self-assurance) I am Matthew, and before I became a disciple of Jesus, I worked for the Roman government collecting taxes. I used to take advantage of one of the "perks" of this profession—skimming a little off the top for personal use. Listening to Jesus, I have come to realize that I have committed a sin against my neighbors. *(in shame)* I took advantage of those people; I cheated them! I became wealthy by stealing their hard-earned wages and goods. I hoarded earthly treasures instead of seeking eternal ones. *(looking at Jesus lovingly)* My heart has changed because of Jesus—I even threw a huge feast at my home and invited others who worked in that corrupt organization to meet Him, *(hopeful)* and perhaps be changed as well. *(darkening)* But now that He speaks of a traitor among us, will the others suspect me, a known publican, a sinner? *(sit; to Jesus, contrite)* Lord, is it I?

Monologue: Simon, the Zealot

(intense) Before Jesus called me, I was a member of the Zealots. We believe in God and that God alone rules over this holy nation of Israel, and we refused to pay homage *(pause, look suspiciously at Matthew)* or taxes to any Roman governor. *(sigh)* It goes against my nature, but Jesus teaches that God ordains all powers and governments on earth, allowing them to rule over us, and we must give our due and treat them with respect. Since following the Christ, I have tried to channel my zeal into telling others about Jesus, God's Son, and reaching out to people for His Kingdom.

Is there a spy among us? A Roman, perhaps? *(look at others)* How could any follower of Jesus question His power and authority? *(confidently)* He is God! He is our King! He is greater than any government! Could I somehow revert to my old ways—could I, Simon, betray my King? *(sit; to Jesus)* Is it I?

King Triumphant

SATB

Ruth Elaine Schram

Duration: 1:50

www.lorenz.com

11
Bless - ed is He who comes in the Name of the Lord, who comes in the Name of the
13
17
Lord!
We know the
15
proph - e - cy of Zech - a - ri - ah, we know the

17
prom - ise that was fore - told, that we would see our bless - ed Mes-
18
20
poco rall.
si - ah, that He would be rid-ing on a colt! Here He
poco rall.
23
a tempo
comes! The King Tri - um - phant! Ho - san - na to the Son of Da - vid!
a tempo

25
Bless - ed is He who comes in the Name of the Lord, who comes in the Name of the
27
Lord!
We throw our
29
cloaks and our coats be - fore Him, we lay the

31
branch - es at His feet. We wave the palms as we a -
34
poco rall.
dore Him, it is the Prom - ised One we
poco rall.
19
36
a tempo
greet! Here He comes! The King Tri - um - phant! Ho -
The King Tri - um - phant! Hail to the
a tempo

38
san - na to the Son of Da - vid! Bless-ed is He who comes in the Name of the
King, the Son of Da - vid!
40
ff
Lord, who comes in the Name of the Lord. He comes in the Name of the
ff
42
Lord!

Monologue: Bartholomew/Nathanael

(with conviction) I'm known as Bartholomew to some, Nathanael to others. I've been a diligent student of the scriptures and a disciple of John, the Baptizer. My friend Philip told me about this Jesus of Nazareth, saying He was the one about whom the prophets had written. At first, I was skeptical. Jesus—of Nazareth? *(with disgust)* Filthy, immoral place. Can anything good come out of Nazareth? *(with wonder)* But John said Jesus was "the Lamb of God, who takes away the sin of the world."

(slowly) Then I met this Jesus. *(with amazement)* He seemed to know me already, to know my innermost thoughts. Although I have always been a devout man, I realized Jesus was offering something more intimate, more personal than my religion ever offered before. For over a thousand years, we have been celebrating the Feast of Passover, *(point to bowl of saltwater)* remembering the bitter slavery in Egypt with the bitter herbs, *(gesture toward wine)* remembering the ten plagues with the ten drops from the goblet. Remembering how the blood of the sacrificed lamb caused the angel of death to pass over the Israelites and spare their firstborn. *(smiling)* Remembering how God set His people free. That wonderful story! How they fled with no time to cook leavened bread—they baked unleavened bread in the warmth of the sun. *(wondering)* Now Jesus breaks this unleavened bread and says, "This is my body." He shares the cup and says, "This is my blood. Do this in remembrance of me."

I don't understand. *(sit slowly; more quietly)* What could make me betray my Friend? *(to Jesus, honestly questioning)* Lord, is it I?

Monologue: Philip

My name is Philip. Jesus came to me one day when I was working and said simply, "Follow me." I spent an entire day with Him, and I was convinced—*(excited)* this is truly the Promised One! It has taken some time for me to understand that this Man, this fulfilled promise, is actually...God, here, among us!

Recently, thousands of men and women, families, were sitting on the hillside, listening to Him teach. Jesus asked me where we could buy bread to feed them all. *(a little embarrassed)* At once, I thought only of the actual, physical cost of such a venture—why, our treasury does not hold such funds! I gave no thought to the people's discomfort, or to the possibility of a divine miracle. But Jesus, oh! *(remembering with wonder)* Jesus took five tiny pieces of bread and two tiny fish, prayed over them, and broke them into pieces. He fed thousands, and we collected twelve baskets full of leftovers! *(amazed, looking at Jesus)* God, here, among us.

(confused, looking at each man) Who would deny the Promised One, this divine presence in our midst? And to whom would this person deliver Jesus—to the vain and arrogant priests who refuse to believe God has kept His promise, or to the pagan Roman government that fears a rival Ruler? Could any one of us forget His power, His compassion—could I forget? *(sit; to Jesus, humbled)* Is it I?

Monologue: Thaddaeus/Lebbaeus

(awe-struck, looking at Jesus) His hands. Carpenter hands. Rough, weathered hands...and yet so gentle and loving. His hands reached out and touched a leper, and the disease was erased from his body. His hands reached out and touched Peter's mother-in-law, and her fever disappeared. His hands reached out and lifted Jairus's daughter from her deathbed. His hands opened the ears of the deaf and the eyes of the blind and mended the bones of the lame. *(emphatically)* Countless infirmities, illnesses, deformities—gone.

(gently; reaching out) His hands reached out, blessing little children when others would have turned them aside. *(reaching down)* His hands reached down, rescuing Peter out of a churning sea that would have swallowed him. *(looking at Jesus; folding hands in front)* His hands, blessing and breaking bread, folding in prayer. Such simple gestures, and yet... *(open hands palm up and study them)* so profound. Those hands that have shown mercy and kindness, *(bowing head)* given love and healing; *(with wonder; gesture around table)* those hands that served me, Thaddaeus, and His other brothers, *(gesture upward)* and worshipped His Father: they are the hands of God in this very room.

(looking around the room) All of us have received blessing from His hands. All of us have seen the miracles those hands have performed. Who could betray Him into the hands of an enemy? *(looking at Jesus; quietly sit)* Will I, Thaddaeus, betray You? *(more softly)* Is it I?

His Hands

SATB

Ruth Elaine Schram

Duration: 4:00

www.lorenz.com

14
22
mf
His
ev - er gen - tle, ev - er kind.
17
dim.
fin - gers, learn - ing, chang - ing, as He grew from boy to
mf
dim.
20
mp
poco rall. e dim.
p
man; His hands, flesh and blood, yet di -
mp
poco rall. e dim.
p

23
a tempo
23
mp
vine.
His
a tempo
mp
mf
27
hands
knew the rough-ness of the wood, knew the tex-ture of the
wood,
the
mp
30
cresc.
grain,
work-ing hands
knew each curve and ev - 'ry
grain,
cresc.

33
24
mf
line.
The car - pen-ter's ap -
mf
36
pren - tice, gain-ing skill with wood and nail; His
39
poco rall. e dim.
mp a tempo
hands, flesh and blood, yet di - vine.
poco rall. e dim.
mp a tempo

25
42
mf
His hands blessed the bread, and the
mf
45
mul - ti-tude was fed. His touch turned the
48
26
wa - ter in - to wine. His

51
cresc.
f
3
hands reached out as He said, "Laz - a - rus come back from the
3
3
cresc.
f
54
poco rall.
dead!" All pow'r on earth is His to com-mand with heav-en's voice, heav-en's
to com-mand with heav-en's
poco rall.
27
57
mf
mp
a tempo
hands, His hands. His hands
hands, His hands. His hands, lov - ing
mf
mp
a tempo

60
hum-bly washed the dust - y feet of His dis - ci - ples, one by one, washed the
hands, washed the dust - y feet of His dis - ci - ples, one by one, washed the
63
cresc.
28
feet that those ver - y hands de - signed.
feet, dust - y feet those ver - y hands de - signed.
cresc.
66
f
Those hands that serve and lend, hands that
f

29
69
mf
poco rall.
cure and heal and mend, Je - sus' hands will bear the
mf
poco rall.
72
rit.
mp
scars meant for mine, meant for mine; His
rit.
75
slowly
hands, flesh and blood, yet di - vine.
slowly
mp
p

Monologue: John

I am John, the "beloved" disciple. *(humbly, with awe)* Beloved! Loved by Jesus! Loved by the One who was in the beginning with God. Loved by the One who is greater than all of us, and yet washes our feet, setting an example of humility and servitude.

You might think that because Jesus calls me His beloved disciple that I have reason to be proud. *(bowing head in humility)* Oh, how I have learned that the opposite is true. I once thought that I might hold a place of power and prestige in His Kingdom, but He has shown me over and over that the war He wages is a spiritual battle. He reaches out to the needy, paupers—He does not seek out the rich and powerful. He dines in the homes of sinners and common folk, not the elite. I have seen Him equally befriend a well-known Pharisee and an immoral woman, forgiving both. *(more emphatically)* God has sent His Son because He loved the world—*(softer)* the lowly—*(very softly)* me—so much. So much that He does not want any one of us to perish, but to have everlasting life. This Jesus, He is the way, the truth; *(slowly, emphasize each word)* He is Life.

(looking around at others) Even though we are His closest friends and followers, I don't think we truly understand the depth of His love. I believe He would give His life for mine. How could I not do the same? *(tearfully)* Will my pride cause me to stumble—will I betray Him? Could I? *(sit; quietly, to Jesus)* Is it I?

Monologue: Thomas

(with a critical manner) I have been listening to Jesus speak tonight around this table, and I simply do not understand. Words meant to comfort, but words met with confusion and misunderstanding. Talk of betrayal, met with incredulity and suspicion. *(frustrated)* Where is He going? *(emphatically)* There is so much yet to be done, right here, right now!

(in awe and wonder) Sometimes I marvel that I, Thomas, have seen Him with my own eyes! *(look at hands)* I have touched my Lord and Master with my own hands. *(look at Jesus)* I have watched Him perform wonders, change lives. *(confused)* I don't want Him to go away, not now, not ever. And how can we follow Him if we don't know where He is going? *(becoming more contrite)* Is there something I have done or will do that will contribute to this betrayal He speaks of? *(inward; clutching heart)* Has He seen my lack of faith, my hidden doubts, my fear? *(sit; to Jesus)* Is it I?

Monologue: Judas Iscariot

(emotionally charged throughout) I am Judas Iscariot, the treasurer for this group. I have followed Jesus, but I am growing tired of his reluctance to take a stand against our oppressors. I believe He is who He says He is, but why would God send a Messiah for this—*(with disgust)* to wash feet and serve bread? I have no need of a "spiritual" king! *(emphatically)* We need a political king, *(shake fists)* someone to rise up and overthrow these Roman tyrants! Thousands of people follow Him over mountainsides and across rivers to hear Him speak; surely He could put together an army in no time. Something must be done to force Him to make His move, to lead us to victory, to establish the New Kingdom!

(look at others with distaste) A betrayer among us, indeed. All these men look at one another suspiciously around this table, wondering, guessing, accusing. They look inwardly and ponder their own motivations, *(growing more frustrated)* but why do they sit here like sheep waiting for a shepherd? Someone must DO something! Well, I have.

Tonight the elders and chief priests will help me help Him usher in the promised Kingdom. History will thank me for this! *(quietly)* Oh yes, someone has betrayed Him. *(sit)* Perhaps all of us will do so before this night is over. *(to Jesus, with mock innocence)* Master, is it I? *(Judas picks up a small pouch jingling with coins, looks at Jesus a bit guiltily and exits.)*

You Are the Bread*

SATB

Ruth Elaine Schram

[30] **Freely** ♩ = ca. 69

mf

5

[31] **Thoughtfully** ♩ = 96

rit.

10

SA *mf*

We come to Your ta - ble, to take of the

TB

*A communion service may be inserted here. See page 64 for optional serving suggestions.

Duration: 3:50

www.lorenz.com

14
bread and the wine.
We come to Your
19
di - vine.
32
ta - ble, to know You, to share the di - vine, di -
24
vine. To hear once a - gain of Your grace, of the

28
Pass - o - ver lamb, sac - ri - fice, and re - demp - tion, Your
32
mer - ci - ful plan from be - fore time be - gan, from be -
36
33
poco rall.
fore time be - gan.
be - gan, be - fore time be - gan.
be - gan.
poco rall.

a tempo

40 mp You are the bread;

You are the bread; **Bless - ed art Thou, O Lord our God, King of the*

mp *a tempo*

44 You are the bread.

un - i-verse, Who bring - est forth bread from the earth.

34

48 mf

You are the Bread of Life; take and eat, nev-er

mf

*The italicized text is an actual Passover blessing that has been recited for thirty-five centuries in the Passover celebration. This is a direct translation of what Jesus would have said at the Last Supper when He blessed the bread and broke it.

52

a - gain.

poco rall.

35

hun - ger a - gain, nev-er hun - ger a - gain.

a - gain, a - gain.

a - gain.

poco rall.

64
You are the wine, the blood that is shed;
68
poco rall.
36
cresc.
You are the bread. You are the bread.
the bread.
poco rall.
cresc.
mf
a tempo
72
You are the bread; Bless - ed art Thou, O Lord our God,
You are the bread; Bless - ed art Thou, O Lord our God, King of the
mf
a tempo

76
You are the bread.
un - i-verse, Who bring - est forth bread from the earth.
80
You are the Bread of Life; take and eat, nev-er
37
84
a - gain.
poco rall.
hun - ger a - gain, nev-er hun - ger a - gain.
a - gain, a - gain.
poco rall.

a tempo
88
You are the wine; Bless - ed art Thou, O Lord our God,
You are the wine; Bless - ed art Thou, O Lord our God, King of the
a tempo
92
You are the wine.
38
un - i - verse, Cre - a - tor of the fruit of the vine.
96
You are the wine, the blood that is shed;

100
rit.
You are the bread.
the bread, You are the bread.
rit.
slowly
mp
104
rit.
freely
You are the wine, the blood that is shed; You are the
slowly
8va
mp
rit.
freely
109
As at first
p
bread.
As at first ♩ = ca. 69
p
pp

How Great His Love (Finale)

SATB

Ruth Elaine Schram

Duration: 1:50

www.lorenz.com

8
Lamb, His pre - cious Son, to die for
10
poco rall.
us, to pur-chase our sal - va - tion. How great His
poco rall.
12
40
love, how great His love for us! How great His

14
a tempo
love, how great His love, that He should
a tempo
16
poco rall.
call us His chil - dren, that He should give
poco rall.
41
19
mf
Je - sus; How great His
How great His
mf

22
a tempo
poco rall.
love, how great His love for
love for us, how great His love,
a tempo
poco rall.
24
a tempo
rit.
mp
42
us, for us.
a tempo
rit.
mp
27
slowly
pp
How great His love!
8va
slowly
pp

Set and Props Suggestions

Set:

- Backdrop: use Da Vinci's painting *The Last Supper* for reference.

  If desired, the Production Support CD-ROM (99/2069L) includes a background-only image of Da Vinci's painting suitable for projecting as a backdrop or for use in creating a custom-made backdrop. (The CD-ROM also includes templates for creating your own programs and posters that coordinate with the cantata artwork, as well as anthem texts suitable for projection during the presentation.)

- Long, low table covered with plain cloth
- 13 low chairs, stools, or cushions behind table, facing congregation

Props:

- Candles and candlesticks
- Goblets
- Decanters and earthen, clay or stoneware jugs of red wine or juice
- White linen or cloth napkins or traditional Passover matzo covers
- Central plate or platter with traditional Last Supper items: lamb bone, flat bread, horseradish, apple relish, roasted egg, parsley or other "bitter" herbs
- Central bowl of saltwater for dipping
- Bowls or plates
- Clusters of grapes
- Flatbread, pita, matzos, or other unleavened bread
- Small bunch of parsley to dip in saltwater; enough for each man to have a taste
- Basin and clean towel for foot washing; may be hidden behind table
- Small pouch filled with coins for Judas

Staging Suggestions and Monologues

Optional Overture/Processional (page 6)

Choir and cast may process into places during the Overture. If Overture is not used for processing, the cast should establish the scene by entering the table area and taking places. Walk and move in a leisurely manner. If desired, a woman dressed in Biblical attire may light candles then exit.

When all are in place, Jesus should pour wine from decanters into goblets, then all should freeze in a picture format.

How Great His Love (page 8)

Jesus, seated in the center, should take three pieces of flatbread and wrap them in clean, white cloth napkins or matzo covers and place them before Him on the table. Then He should pick up the middle piece of bread, hold it up and break it in half, return half to the table, carefully wrap the other half and place it under the table. This hidden piece is referred to as 'His body' in the communion scene.

Monologue: Simon Peter (page 16)

My name is Simon Peter. One day, my partners and I were cleaning our nets after a long, hard night of fishing. We were tired and discouraged; we had nothing to show for our efforts. Jesus was preaching, as usual, to the many people who followed Him from here to there, listening to His every word. He asked if He could sit in my boat, *(gesture outward)* and I rowed Him out a little so His voice would carry. When He had finished teaching, He asked me to row out a little further and throw my nets in the water again. *(becoming agitated)* I told Him it was pointless; we had worked all night and caught nothing! But, I did as He asked. *(with awe)* And then, astonishingly—so many fish—the nets broke trying to pull them in. *(voice rising)* So many fish—we filled both of our ships until they began to sink under the weight of them!

(bowing head) I fell down on my knees before the Lord, feeling sinful and faithless in His Holy presence. Then He told me I would no longer catch fish, but men. I did not fully understand, but I left my boats, my fish, my livelihood—I left everything to follow Jesus, and I have never looked back.

(looking around the table) Tonight He tells us that one of these twelve men, His faithful disciples, will betray Him. *(loudly)* I vainly promised to follow Him even to death, but *(softly)* He looked right into my eyes and said that before the rooster crows, I will deny Him three times. Deny Him! Am I not the "rock" He called me to be? *(emotionally pained)* Could I lose my Lord, my friend, because I am not strong enough to be faithful? *(sit; to Jesus, quietly)* Is it I?

Monologue: Andrew (page 16)

I've been known as "Peter's little brother, Andrew" since the day I was born. Years ago I left the fishing business to follow that fiery preacher, John the Baptizer. He was anointed by God to prepare the way for the long-awaited Messiah, *(look at Jesus)* and now I follow Him.

(smiling) I love to bring people to Jesus. I brought my brother to Jesus, *(look at Peter)* and have watched him grow and become a strong leader among us. *(distant; remembering)* I brought the little boy with the lunch of five loaves and two fish to Jesus. *(look to Jesus)* I have even brought Gentiles to meet the Master because He is open and loving to anyone who is searching for the truth.

(sobering) But Jesus has enemies in high places, enemies who would love to silence Him, or even see Him die. And He speaks of a betrayer in our midst. *(prayerfully)* Oh, please do not let it be me who brings sorrow to my Lord! *(sit; barely audible, to Jesus)* Jesus, is it I?

Monologue: James, the Lesser (page 17)

(a bit reserved) I am James, the Lesser, known as such to describe my stature and to differentiate me from the many other men named James. Since joining Jesus' group of followers, I have seen the most miraculous things! Jesus has the power to calm the sea—even the wind and rain obey His voice. Jesus has power over demons—He has cast out evil spirits and given us the power to do the same in His name. He has the power of healing—He has taken away diseases that people have suffered with for years, even *(in amazement)* from birth. *(with wonder)* Beyond this, He has the power to forgive sin.

(looking at each of several men, studying their faces, end with back to Jesus) And now one of these men at this dinner table, one who eats and drinks with Him, will betray Him. How could anyone doubt that He is the Lord, our Messiah, after walking and talking with Him, after seeing prophecies fulfilled, and miracle after miracle, proof after proof? He has called each of us to follow—*(turn to Jesus)* who could turn away? *(sit)* Is it I?

Is It I? (page 18)

Characters freeze scene in picture format. During last chorus, Jesus and the disciples should break their freeze and Jesus should dip a small piece of parsley into saltwater; each of the disciples should do the same. Judas's hand should dip just after Jesus; their hands will be in the bowl at the same time. After all the disciples taste the bitter parsley, freeze in picture format.

Monologue: James, the son of Zebedee (page 25)

(with some arrogance) My name is James; *(gesture toward John)* John is my younger brother. We used to work with Peter and Andrew in the fishing industry. Jesus called us to follow Him on the same day that He called Peter, *(look toward Peter)*

and we did, thinking that He would establish His kingdom on earth and that we would be His right-hand men.

Jesus calls John and me *(enjoying the title)* "the Sons of Thunder!" *(aside)* Actually, we are the sons of Zebedee, a rich and powerful man in this community who is a personal friend of some of the more influential religious leaders. At one time, I had hoped that this would assure me of a position of power in the new kingdom. In fact, my mother suggested I should sit at Jesus' right hand when He claimed His throne, *(look at John)* and John at His left. *(with authority)* After all, it was we who were invited to the mountain with Jesus, and we saw Him transfigured. *(looking up)* His face shone like the sun, *(with wonder)* and the voice of God spoke out of heaven.

(looking out again) He chose me! He chose each of us. How could one of us betray Him? We have seen His perfect adherence to the law; we have heard the voice of God say, "this is My Son." We have been present during countless miracles, healings—works no mere man could accomplish. *(gesture to John)* Could it be my brother, John? *(look around the table; sit)* Could it be me? *(to Jesus)* Is it I?

Monologue: Matthew (page 25)

(with strength and self-assurance) I am Matthew, and before I became a disciple of Jesus, I worked for the Roman government collecting taxes. I used to take advantage of one of the "perks" of this profession—skimming a little off the top for personal use. Listening to Jesus, I have come to realize that I have committed a sin against my neighbors. *(in shame)* I took advantage of those people; I cheated them! I became wealthy by stealing their hard-earned wages and goods. I hoarded earthly treasures instead of seeking eternal ones. *(looking at Jesus lovingly)* My heart has changed because of Jesus—I even threw a huge feast at my home and invited others who worked in that corrupt organization to meet Him, (hopeful) and perhaps be changed as well. *(darkening)* But now that He speaks of a traitor among us, will the others suspect me, a known publican, a sinner? *(sit; to Jesus, contrite)* Lord, is it I?

Monologue: Simon, the Zealot (page 25)

(intense) Before Jesus called me, I was a member of the Zealots. We believe in God and that God alone rules over this holy nation of Israel, and we refused to pay homage *(pause, look suspiciously at Matthew)* or taxes to any Roman governor. *(sigh)* It goes against my nature, but Jesus teaches that God ordains all powers and governments on earth, allowing them to rule over us, and we must give our due and treat them with respect. Since following the Christ, I have tried to channel my zeal into telling others about Jesus, God's Son, and reaching out to people for His Kingdom.

Is there a spy among us? A Roman, perhaps? *(look at others)* How could any follower of Jesus question His power and authority? *(confidently)* He is God! He is God! He is our King! He is greater than any government! Could I somehow revert to my old ways—could I, Simon, betray my King? *(sit; to Jesus)* Is it I?

King Triumphant (page 26)

Characters freeze in picture format. During last chorus, Jesus should break His freeze and take the hidden piece of bread from beneath the table, remove the napkin, break the bread into pieces and give one to each disciple. As Jesus distributes the bread, the disciples should break their freeze and eat the bread. Jesus should drip ten drops from his wine goblet onto a plate, then take a sip and pass the cup to each disciple, who in turn should take a sip.

Monologue: Bartholomew/Nathanael (page 32)

(with conviction) I'm known as Bartholomew to some, Nathanael to others. I've been a diligent student of the scriptures and a disciple of John, the Baptizer. My friend Philip told me about this Jesus of Nazareth, saying He was the one about whom the prophets had written. At first, I was skeptical. Jesus—of Nazareth? *(with disgust)* Filthy, immoral place. Can anything good come out of Nazareth? *(with wonder)* But John said Jesus was "the Lamb of God, who takes away the sin of the world."

(slowly) Then I met this Jesus. *(with amazement)* He seemed to know me already, to know my innermost thoughts. Although I have always been a devout man, I realized Jesus was offering something more intimate, more personal than my religion ever offered before. For over a thousand years, we have been celebrating the Feast of Passover, *(point to bowl of saltwater)* remembering the bitter slavery in Egypt with the bitter herbs, *(gesture toward wine)* remembering the ten plagues with the ten drops from the goblet. Remembering how the blood of the sacrificed lamb caused the angel of death to pass over the Israelites and spare their firstborn. (smiling) Remembering how God set His people free. That wonderful story! How they fled with no time to cook leavened bread—they baked unleavened bread in the warmth of the sun. *(wondering)* Now Jesus breaks this unleavened bread and says, "This is my body." He shares the cup and says, "This is my blood. Do this in remembrance of me."

I don't understand. *(sit slowly; more quietly)* What could make me betray my Friend? *(to Jesus, honestly questioning)* Lord, is it I?

Monologue: Philip (page 32)

My name is Philip. Jesus came to me one day when I was working and said simply, "Follow me." I spent an entire day with Him, and I was convinced—*(excited)* this is truly the Promised One! It has taken some time for me to understand that this Man, this fulfilled promise, is actually...God, here, among us!

Recently, thousands of men and women, families, were sitting on the hillside, listening to Him teach. Jesus asked me where we could buy bread to feed them all. *(a little embarrassed)* At once, I thought only of the actual, physical cost of such a venture—why, our treasury does not hold such funds! I gave no thought to the people's discomfort, or to the possibility of a divine miracle. But Jesus, oh! *(remembering with wonder)* Jesus took five tiny pieces of bread and two tiny fish, prayed over them, and broke them into pieces. He fed thousands, and we collected twelve baskets full of leftovers! *(amazed, looking at Jesus)* God, here, among us.

(confused, looking at each man) Who would deny the Promised One, this divine presence in our midst? And to whom would this person deliver Jesus—to the vain and arrogant priests who refuse to believe God has kept His promise, or to the pagan Roman government that fears a rival Ruler? Could any one of us forget His power, His compassion—could I forget? *(sit; to Jesus, humbled)* Is it I?

Monologue: Thaddaeus/Lebbaeus (page 33)

(awe-struck, looking at Jesus) His hands. Carpenter hands. Rough, weathered hands...and yet so gentle and loving. His hands reached out and touched a leper, and the disease was erased from his body. His hands reached out and touched Peter's mother-in-law, and her fever disappeared. His hands reached out and lifted Jairus's daughter from her deathbed. His hands opened the ears of the deaf and the eyes of the blind and mended the bones of the lame. *(emphatically)* Countless infirmities, illnesses, deformities—gone.

(gently; reaching out) His hands reached out, blessing little children when others would have turned them aside. *(reaching down)* His hands reached down, rescuing Peter out of a churning sea that would have swallowed him. *(looking at Jesus; folding hands in front)* His hands, blessing and breaking bread, folding in prayer. Such simple gestures, and yet... *(open hands palm up and study them)* so profound. Those hands that have shown mercy and kindness, *(bowing head)* given love and healing; *(with wonder; gesture around table)* those hands that served me, Thaddaeus, and His other brothers, *(gesture upward)* and worshipped His Father: they are the hands of God in this very room.

(looking around the room) All of us have received blessing from His hands. All of us have seen the miracles those hands have performed. Who could betray Him into the hands of an enemy? *(looking at Jesus; quietly sit)* Will I, Thaddaeus, betray You? *(more softly)* Is it I?

His Hands (page 34)

When the song begins, Jesus should take a basin and towel and wash each of the disciples' feet in turn. They may mime conversations with Him and interact quietly with one another. When Jesus finishes washing John's feet, the two should embrace briefly. Jesus should then return to middle seat and all freeze in picture format.

Monologue: John (page 42)

I am John, the "beloved" disciple. *(humbly, with awe)* Beloved! Loved by Jesus! Loved by the One who was in the beginning with God. Loved by the One who is greater than all of us, and yet washes our feet, setting an example of humility and servitude.

You might think that because Jesus calls me His beloved disciple that I have reason to be proud. *(bowing head in humility)* Oh, how I have learned that the opposite is true. I once thought that I might hold a place of power and prestige in His Kingdom, but He has shown me over and over that the war He wages is a spiritual battle. He reaches out to the needy, paupers—He does not seek out the rich and powerful. He dines in the homes of sinners and common folk, not the elite. I have seen Him equally befriend a well-known Pharisee and an immoral woman, forgiving both. *(more emphatically)* God has sent His Son because He loved the world—*(softer)* the lowly—*(very softly)* me—so much. So much that He does not want any one of us to perish, but to have everlasting life. This Jesus, He is the way, the truth; *(slowly, emphasize each word)* He is Life.

(looking around at others) Even though we are His closest friends and followers, I don't think we truly understand the depth of His love. I believe He would give His life for mine. How could I not do the same? *(tearfully)* Will my pride cause me to stumble—will I betray Him? Could I? *(sit; quietly, to Jesus)* Is it I?

Monologue: Thomas (page 42)

(with a critical manner) I have been listening to Jesus speak tonight around this table, and I simply do not understand. Words meant to comfort, but words met with confusion and misunderstanding. Talk of betrayal, met with incredulity and suspicion. *(frustrated)* Where is He going? *(emphatically)* There is so much yet to be done, right here, right now!

(in awe and wonder) Sometimes I marvel that I, Thomas, have seen Him with my own eyes! *(look at hands)* I have touched my Lord and Master with my own hands. *(look at Jesus)* I have watched Him perform wonders, change lives. *(confused)* I don't want Him to go away, not now, not ever. And how can we follow Him if we don't know where He is going? *(becoming more contrite)* Is there something I have done or will do that will contribute to this betrayal He speaks of? *(inward; clutching heart)* Has He seen my lack of faith, my hidden doubts, my fear? *(sit; to Jesus)* Is it I?

Monologue: Judas Iscariot (page 43)

(emotionally charged throughout) I am Judas Iscariot, the treasurer for this group. I have followed Jesus, but I am growing tired of his reluctance to take a stand against our oppressors. I believe He is who He says He is, but why would God send a Messiah for this—*(with disgust)* to wash feet and serve bread? I have no need of a "spiritual" king! *(emphatically)* We need a political king, *(shake fists)* someone to rise up and overthrow these Roman tyrants! Thousands of people

follow Him over mountainsides and across rivers to hear Him speak; surely He could put together an army in no time. Something must be done to force Him to make His move, to lead us to victory, to establish the New Kingdom!

(look at others with distaste) A betrayer among us, indeed. All these men look at one another suspiciously around this table, wondering, guessing, accusing. They look inwardly and ponder their own motivations, *(growing more frustrated)* but why do they sit here like sheep waiting for a shepherd? Someone must DO something! Well, I have.

Tonight the elders and chief priests will help me help Him usher in the promised Kingdom. History will thank me for this! *(quietly)* Oh yes, someone has betrayed Him. *(sit)* Perhaps all of us will do so before this night is over. *(to Jesus, with mock innocence)* Master, is it I?

(Judas picks up a small pouch jingling with coins, looks at Jesus a bit guiltily and exits.)

You Are the Bread (page 44)

During this anthem, an optional communion service for the congregation may be observed. If time and space permit, have the congregation come to the Last Supper table by processing from the outside of the pews, one person stopping in front of each disciple. The disciple should break off a piece of unleavened bread and hand it to the person closest to him; the congregants then walk toward the center of the table, dipping the piece of bread into the cup Jesus holds. After partaking, have the congregation return to their seats by the inside of the pew (from the center aisle). This will keep the lines moving in one direction and keep people in the order in which they were seated.

If desired, the disciples or the man portraying Jesus may quietly repeat "The body of Christ, broken for you, the blood of Christ, shed for you."

If desired, the minister may speak or deliver a short meditation at this time.

How Great His Love (Finale) (page 53)